FAMOUS AMERICANS

CD-ROM AND BOOK

450 Portraits from Colonial Times to 1900

DOVER PUBLICATIONS, INC.
Mineola, New York

D1122272

This book contains portraits of 450 individuals born before 1900, who contributed to American life in some vital way.

Bibliographical Note

Famous Americans CD-ROM and Book: 450 Portraits from Colonial Times to 1900, first published by Dover Publications, Inc. in 2005, is a new selection of designs from *Dictionary of American Portraits: 4045 Pictures of Important Americans from Earliest Times to the Beginning of the Twentieth Century,* originally published by Dover Publications, Inc., in 1967.

Dover Electronic Clip Art®

International Standard Book Number: 0-486-99654-9

Manufactured in the United States of America
Dover Publications, Inc., 31 East 2nd Street, Mineola, N.Y. 11501

The CD-ROM on the inside back cover contains all of the images shown in the book. There is no installation necessary. Just insert the CD into your computer and call the images into your favorite software (refer to the documentation with your software for further instructions). Each image has been saved in three different formats-300 dpi grayscale TIFF, high-resolution JPEG, and 72-dpi Internet-ready JPEG.

The "Images" folder on the CD contains a number of different folders. All of the TIFF images have been placed in one folder, as have all of the high-resolution JPEG, and all of the Internet-ready JPEG. The images in each of these folders are identical except for file format. Every image has a unique file name in the following format: xxx.xxx. The first 3 characters of the file name, before the period, correspond to the number printed with the image. The last 3 characters of the file name, after the period, refer to the file format. So, 001.TIF would be the first file in the TIFF folder.

Also included on the CD-ROM is Dover Design Manager, a simple graphics editing program for Windows that will allow you to view, print, crop, and rotate the images.

For technical support, contact:
  Telephone: 1 (617) 249-0245
  Fax: 1 (617) 249-0245
  Email: dover@artimaging.com
  Internet: **http://www.dovertechsupport.com**
  The fastest way to receive technical support is via email or the Internet.

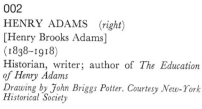

001
ABIGAIL ADAMS *(left)*
[Mrs. John Adams, nee Abigail Smith]
(1744–1818)
First lady, 1797–1801
Painting by Gilbert Stuart

002
HENRY ADAMS *(right)*
[Henry Brooks Adams]
(1838–1918)
Historian, writer; author of *The Education
of Henry Adams*
*Drawing by John Briggs Potter. Courtesy New-York
Historical Society*

003
JOHN ADAMS *(left)*
(1735–1826)
President of the United States, 1797–1801
Painting by Charles Willson Peale. Courtesy Independence National Historical Park

004
JOHN QUINCY ADAMS *(right)*
(1767–1848)
President of the United States, 1825–1829
*Engraved by W. Wellstood after a photograph by
Mathew Brady*

005
Mrs. JOHN QUINCY ADAMS *(left)*
[nee Louisa Catherine Johnson]
(1775–1852)
First lady, 1825–1829
Painting by Gilbert Stuart

006
SAMUEL ADAMS *(right)*
(1722–1803)
Revolutionary patriot, signer of Declaration
of Independence
Painting by John Singleton Copley

007
JANE ADDAMS *(left)*
(1860–1935)
Social reformer, founder of Hull House,
Nobel Peace Laureate

008
LOUIS AGASSIZ *(right)*
[Jean Louis Rodolphe Agassiz]
(1807–1873)
Naturalist, biologist, ichthyologist, writer,
educator
Courtesy Burndy Library

009
LOUISA MAY ALCOTT *(left)*
(1832–1888)
Novelist, author of juvenile books

010
HORATIO ALGER *(right)*
(1832–1899)
Author of boys' stories

011
WASHINGTON ALLSTON *(left)*
(1779–1843)
Painter, writer
Painting by Gilbert Stuart

012
ROBERT ANDERSON *(right)*
(1805–1871)
Union officer, commanded Fort Sumter
Courtesy New-York Historical Society

013
SUSAN BROWNELL ANTHONY
(*left*)
(1820–1906)
Woman-suffrage leader
Courtesy Tamiment Institute Library

014
BENEDICT ARNOLD   (*right*)
(1741–1801)
Revolutionary officer; traitor
Engraving by Henry B. Hall

015
CHESTER ALAN ARTHUR   (*left*)
(1830–1886)
President of the United States, 1881–1885
Courtesy New-York Historical Society

016
Mrs. CHESTER A. ARTHUR   (*right*)
[nee Ellen Lewis Herndon]
(1837–1880)
Wife of Chester A. Arthur, died before he
took office
Courtesy Library of Congress

017
JOHN JACOB ASTOR   (*left*)
(1864–1912)
Capitalist, inventor

018
Mrs. WILLIAM ASTOR   (*right*)
[nee Caroline Webster Schermerhorn]
(1831–1908)
New York society leader

019
JOHN JAMES AUDUBON (*left*)
(1785–1851)
Ornithologist, artist, naturalist, writer
Courtesy Library of Congress, Brady-Handy Collection

020
STEPHEN FULLER AUSTIN (*right*)
(1793–1836)
Colonizer of Texas, son of Moses Austin
Courtesy Texas State Library

021
GEORGE BANCROFT (*left*)
(1800–1891)
Historian, diplomat

022
JOEL BARLOW (*right*)
(1754–1812)
Poet, diplomat; one of "Hartford Wits"
Engraved by A. Smith from a painting by Robert Fulton

023
P. T. BARNUM (*left*)
[Phineas Taylor Barnum]
(1810–1891)
Showman
Courtesy Loan Collection of Elizabeth Sterling Seeley, Barnum Museum

024
ETHEL BARRYMORE (*right*)
(1879–1959)
Actress
Courtesy Walter Hampden Memorial Library at The Players, New York

025
JOHN BARRYMORE *(left)*
(1882–1942)
Actor
Courtesy Walter Hampden Memorial Library at The Players, New York

026
JOHN BARTLETT *(right)*
(1820–1905)
Editor, publisher; compiled *Familiar Quotations*
Courtesy Little, Brown and Co.

027
CLARA BARTON *(left)*
[Clarissa Harlowe Barton]
(1821–1912)
Founder of American Red Cross

028
SAM BASS *(right)*
(1851–1878)
Western outlaw
Courtesy University of Texas Library

029
LYMAN FRANK BAUM *(left)*
(1856–1919)
Writer, author of *The Wizard of Oz*
Courtesy Fred Meyer

030
ROY BEAN *(right)*
(c. 1825–1903)
Western judge

031
DAN BEARD   (*left*)
[Daniel Carter Beard]
(1850–1941)
Writer, illustrator; organized first American
Boy Scout group
Photograph by Pach Brothers

032
PIERRE GUSTAVE TOUTANT DE
BEAUREGARD   (*right*)
(1818–1893)
Confederate general, commanded bom-
bardment of Fort Sumter
Courtesy New-York Historical Society

033
HENRY WARD BEECHER   (*left*)
(1813–1887)
Congregational clergyman, orator, aboli-
tionist, reformer
Engraving by George E. Perine

034
DAVID BELASCO   (*right*)
(1854–1931)
Theatrical producer, playwright

035
ALEXANDER GRAHAM BELL   (*left*)
(1847–1922)
Inventor, educator of the deaf

036
EDWARD BELLAMY   (*right*)
(1850–1898)
Writer, author of *Looking Backward*

037
THOMAS HART BENTON (*left*)
["Old Bullion" Benton]
(1782–1858)
U.S. Senator
Engraving by John Rogers

038
LOUISE BETHUNE (*right*)
[nee Louise Blanchard]
(1856–1913)
First woman architect in U.S.

039
AMBROSE GWINNETT BIERCE
(*left*)
(1842–c. 1914)
Author, journalist
Courtesy California Historical Society

040
ALBERT BIERSTADT (*right*)
(1830–1902)
Painter

041
BILLY THE KID (*left*)
[William H. Bonney]
(1859–1881)
Western outlaw

042
GEORGE CALEB BINGHAM (*right*)
(1811–1879)
Genre and portrait painter; state official
Self-portrait. Courtesy School District, Kansas City, Missouri

Bingham 7

043
BLACK HAWK (*left*)
[Ma-ka-tae-mish-kia-kiak]
(1767–1838)
Sac (Sauk) Indian chief

044
NELLIE BLY (*right*)
[Elizabeth Seaman; nee Elizabeth
Cochrane]
(1867–1922)
Journalist; traveled around world in 72 days
to outdo Verne's Phileas Fogg

045
DANIEL BOONE (*left*)
(1734–1820)
Pioneer
*Engraved by James B. Longacre from a painting by
Chester Harding*

046
EDWIN THOMAS BOOTH (*right*)
(1833–1893)
Actor
Courtesy New-York Historical Society

047
JOHN WILKES BOOTH (*left*)
(1838–1865)
Actor, assassin of Abraham Lincoln
Courtesy New-York Historical Society

048
LIZZIE ANDREW BORDEN (*right*)
(1860–1927)
Defendant in murder trial, Fall River,
Massachusetts, 1892; acquitted

049
JAMES BOWIE *(left)*
(c. 1796–1836)
Texas soldier, reputed originator of Bowie knife
Courtesy Texas State Library

050
BELLE BOYD *(right)*
[Belle Boyd Hardinge]
(1843–1900)
Confederate spy
Courtesy Confederate Museum

051
DIAMOND JIM BRADY *(left)*
[James Buchanan Brady]
(1856–1917)
Financier, playboy
Courtesy Free Library of Philadelphia

052
MATHEW B. BRADY *(right)*
(c. 1823–1896)
Photographer
Photograph by L. C. Handy

053
BRAXTON BRAGG *(left)*
(1817–1876)
Confederate general
Engraving by John A. O'Neill

054
JOSEPH BRANT *(right)*
[Thayendanegea]
(1742–1807)
Mohawk Indian chief, leader in Cherry Valley massacre
Engraved by John R. Smith from a painting by George Romney. Courtesy New-York Historical Society

055
PHILLIPS BROOKS   (left)
(1835–1893)
Episcopal bishop, author of "O Little Town
of Bethlehem"
Engraving by Thomas Johnson

056
JOHN BROWN   (right)
[John Brown of Osawatomie]
(1800–1859)
Abolitionist, Northern martyr
Courtesy Library of Congress, Brady-Handy Collection

057
WILLIAM JENNINGS BRYAN   (left)
(1860–1925)
Political leader, orator, presidential candidate; Secretary of State under Wilson

058
WILLIAM CULLEN BRYANT   (right)
(1794–1878)
Poet, editor
Photograph by Napoleon Sarony. Courtesy New-York
Historical Society

059
JAMES BUCHANAN   (left)
(1791–1868)
President of the United States, 1857–1861
Engraving by John C. Buttre

060
BUFFALO BILL   (right)
[William Frederick Cody]
(1846–1917)
Western scout, showman
Courtesy New-York Historical Society

061
CHARLES BULFINCH *(left)*
(1763–1844)
Architect
Painting by Mather Brown

062
NED BUNTLINE *(right)*
[Edward Zane Carroll Judson]
(1823–1866)
Adventurer, author of dime novels
Courtesy Mercaldo Archives

063
GELETT BURGESS *(left)*
[Frank Gelett Burgess]
(1866–1951)
Humorist, illustrator, author of "The
Purple Cow"

064
FRANCES HODGSON BURNETT
(right)
[nee Frances Eliza Hodgson]
(1849–1924)
Writer, author of *Little Lord Fauntleroy*

065
AMBROSE EVERETT BURNSIDE
(left)
(1824–1881)
Union general in Civil War; Governor of
Rhode Island, U.S. Senator
Engraving by John C. Buttre

066
AARON BURR *(right)*
(1756–1836)
Politician; U.S. Senator; Vice-President of
U.S., 1801–1805
Painting by Gilbert Stuart

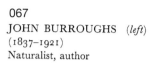

067
JOHN BURROUGHS *(left)*
(1837–1921)
Naturalist, author

068
NICHOLAS MURRAY BUTLER
(right)
(1862–1947)
Educator, president of Columbia University, Nobel Peace Laureate
Courtesy Columbiana Collection, Columbia University

069
GEORGE WASHINGTON CABLE
(left)
(1844–1925)
Writer, author of local-color stories, *Old Creole Days*
Photograph by Napoleon Sarony

070
MOTHER CABRINI *(right)*
[Saint Frances Xavier Cabrini]
(1850–1917)
Roman Catholic nun, charitable leader; canonized in 1946

071
ABRAHAM CAHAN *(left)*
(1860–1951)
Novelist, editor; founded *Jewish Daily Forward*
Courtesy "Jewish Daily Forward"

072
CALAMITY JANE *(right)*
[Martha Jane Burke]
(c. 1852–1903)
Frontier woman, marksman
Courtesy Library of Congress

073
JOHN CALDWELL CALHOUN (*left*)
(1782–1850)
Vice-President of U.S., 1825–1832; U.S.
Senator, Secretary of War, Secretary of
State; political theorist for the South
Daguerreotype by Mathew Brady. Courtesy Library of Congress

074
ANDREW CARNEGIE (*right*)
(1835–1919)
Steel magnate, writer, philanthropist

075
KIT CARSON (*left*)
[Christopher Carson]
(1809–1868)
Trapper, scout, Indian agent
Courtesy Mercaldo Archives

076
GEORGE WASHINGTON CARVER
(*right*)
(1864–1943)
Botanist, educator, known for fundamental
research on the peanut
Courtesy Tuskegee Institute

077
MARY CASSATT (*left*)
(1845–1926)
Painter
Painting by Edgar Degas

078
GEORGE CATLIN (*right*)
(1796–1872)
Painter, writer; early student of the American Indian

079
CHANG AND ENG   (*left*)
[Chang and Eng Bunker]
(1811–1874)
Barnum's Siamese twins
Courtesy Mercaldo Archives

080
WILLIAM MERRITT CHASE   (*right*)
(1849–1916)
Painter

081
CHARLES WADDELL CHESNUTT
(*left*)
(1858–1932)
Writer, lawyer, educator

082
LYDIA CHILD   (*right*)
[nee Lydia Maria Francis]
(1802–1880)
Abolitionist, writer
Engraving by F. T. Stuart

083
FREDERICK EDWIN CHURCH
(*left*)
(1826–1900)
Landscape painter

084
GEORGE ROGERS CLARK   (*right*)
(1752–1818)
Revolutionary officer, conqueror of Old
Northwest
Engraved by Thomas B. Welch from a painting by James B. Longacre after a painting by John Wesley Jarvis

085
WILLIAM CLARK   (*left*)
(1770–1838)
Army officer, explored American Northwest
with Meriwether Lewis
Painting by Charles Willson Peale

086
HENRY CLAY   (*right*)
(1777–1852)
Speaker of the House of Representatives,
U.S. Senator, Secretary of State under J. Q.
Adams; "The Great Compromiser"
*Engraved by W. J. Edwards from a daguerreotype by
Mathew Brady*

087
GROVER CLEVELAND   (*left*)
[Stephen Grover Cleveland]
(1837–1908)
President of the United States, 1885–1889,
1893–1897
Engraving by Henry B. Hall, Jr.

088
Mrs. GROVER CLEVELAND   (*right*)
[nee Frances Folsom]
(1864–1947)
First lady, 1886–1889, 1893–1897
Engraving by John C. Buttre

089
DeWITT CLINTON   (*left*)
(1769–1828)
Mayor of New York City, Governor of New
York; principal promoter of Erie Canal
Painting by Samuel F. B. Morse

090
THOMAS COLE   (*right*)
(1801–1848)
Painter of Hudson River school

091
SAMUEL COLT (*left*)
(1814–1862)
Inventor and manufacturer of the revolver
Engraved by H. W. Smith from a photograph by Mathew Brady

092
CALVIN COOLIDGE (*right*)
[John Calvin Coolidge]
(1872–1933)
President of the United States, 1923–1929
Courtesy Library of Congress

093
Mrs. CALVIN COOLIDGE (*left*)
[nee Grace Anne Goodhue]
(1879–1957)
First lady, 1923–1929
Painting by Howard Chandler Christy. Courtesy Forbes Library

094
JAMES FENIMORE COOPER (*right*)
(1789–1851)
Novelist
Painting by John Wesley Jarvis

095
JOHN SINGLETON COPLEY (*left*)
(1738–1815)
Portrait painter
Self-portrait

096
JAMES JOHN CORBETT (*right*)
["Gentleman Jim" Corbett]
(1866–1933)
Heavyweight boxing champion, defeated John L. Sullivan
Courtesy Mercaldo Archives

097
STEPHEN CRANE *(left)*
(1871–1900)
Novelist, short-story writer, poet, war correspondent
Courtesy Public Library, Newark, New Jersey

098
DAVY CROCKETT *(right)*
[David Crockett]
(1786–1836)
Frontier scout, Congressman; killed at the Alamo
Engraved by Thomas B. Welch from a painting by S. S. Osgood

099
NATHANIEL CURRIER *(left)*
(1813–1888)
Lithographer, partner in Currier and Ives
Courtesy Free Library of Philadelphia

100
GEORGE ARMSTRONG CUSTER
(right)
(1839–1876)
Army officer, killed with all his men in battle of Little Big Horn

101
RICHARD HENRY DANA *(left)*
(1815–1882)
Writer, lawyer, author of *Two Years Before the Mast*

102
CLARENCE SEWARD DARROW
(right)
(1857–1938)
Lawyer
Courtesy Chicago Historical Society

103
JEFFERSON DAVIS   (*left*)
(1808–1889)
President of the Confederacy
Courtesy National Archives, Brady Collection

104
MRS. JEFFERSON DAVIS   (*right*)
[nee Varina Howell]
(1826–1906)
First lady of the Confederacy
Courtesy Confederate Museum

105
RICHARD HARDING DAVIS   (*left*)
(1864–1916)
Reporter, war correspondent, short-story writer, novelist, playwright
Photograph by Napoleon Sarony

106
WILLIAM DAWES   (*right*)
(1745–1799)
Patriot, rode with Paul Revere to Concord, April 18, 1775
Courtesy New-York Historical Society

107
EUGENE VICTOR DEBS   (*left*)
(1855–1926)
Socialist leader
Courtesy Tamiment Institute Library

108
STEPHEN DECATUR   (*right*)
(1779–1820)
Naval officer
Painting by Gilbert Stuart. Courtesy Independence National Historical Park

109
GEORGE DEWEY *(left)*
(1837–1917)
Naval officer in Spanish-American War,
destroyed Spanish squadron at Manila Bay

110
EMILY DICKINSON *(right)*
[Emily Elizabeth Dickinson]
(1830–1886)
Poet

111
MARY MAPES DODGE *(left)*
[nee Mary Elizabeth Mapes]
(1831–1905)
Author of children's books, editor of *St.
Nicholas Magazine*

112
ABNER DOUBLEDAY *(right)*
(1819–1893)
Union general in Civil War; erroneously
credited with invention of baseball
*Engraved by John C. Buttre from a photograph by
Mathew Brady*

113
FREDERICK DOUGLASS *(left)*
[Frederick Augustus Washington Bailey]
(c. 1817–1895)
Abolitionist, lecturer, journalist

114
ANDREW JACKSON DOWNING
(right)
(1815–1852)
Horticulturist, landscape gardener, architect

115

THEODORE DREISER (*left*)
(1871–1945)
Novelist

116

PAUL LAURENCE DUNBAR (*right*)
(1872–1906)
Poet
Courtesy Ohio Historical Society

117

ISADORA DUNCAN (*left*)
(1878–1927)
Dancer
Photograph by Arnold Genthe

118

PIERRE SAMUEL DU PONT DE
NEMOURS (*right*)
(1739–1817)
French economist, printer; father of E. I.
and Victor Marie du Pont
Courtesy E.I. du Pont de Nemours & Co., Inc.

119

THOMAS EAKINS (*left*)
(1844–1916)
Painter, sculptor
Self-portrait

120

JUBAL ANDERSON EARLY (*right*)
(1816–1894)
Confederate general

121
WYATT EARP   *(left)*
[Wyatt Berry Stapp Earp]
(1848–1929)
Western lawman
Courtesy Mercaldo Archives

122
GEORGE EASTMAN   *(right)*
(1854–1932)
Photographic inventor and manufacturer;
founded Eastman Kodak Co. and Eastman
School of Music
Courtesy George Eastman House

123
MARY BAKER EDDY   *(left)*
[nee Mary Morse Baker]
(1821–1910)
Founder of the Christian Science Church;
writer
*Courtesy First Church of Christ Scientist, Boston,
Massachusetts*

124
THOMAS ALVA EDISON   *(right)*
(1847–1931)
Inventor

125
JONATHAN EDWARDS   *(left)*
(1703–1758)
Congregational clergyman, theologian, philosopher

126
DWIGHT DAVID EISENHOWER
(right)
(1890–1969)
President of the United States, 1953–1961
Courtesy Library of Congress

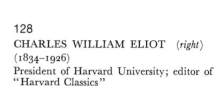

127
Mrs. DWIGHT DAVID EISENHOWER
(*left*)
[nee Mamie Geneva Doud]
(1896–1979)
First lady, 1953–1961
Painting by Thomas E. Stephens. Courtesy White House Collection

128
CHARLES WILLIAM ELIOT   (*right*)
(1834–1926)
President of Harvard University; editor of "Harvard Classics"

129
RALPH WALDO EMERSON   (*left*)
(1803–1882)
Essayist, poet, Transcendentalist, lecturer
Engraving by J. A. J. Wilcox

130
FANNIE FARMER   (*right*)
[Fannie Merritt Farmer]
(1857–1915)
Editor, *Boston Cooking School Cook Book*
Courtesy Little, Brown and Co.

131
DAVID GLASGOW FARRAGUT
(*left*)
(1801–1870)
Union naval officer in Civil War; hero of battle of Mobile Bay

132
EUGENE FIELD   (*right*)
(1850–1895)
Journalist, poet, humorist

133

MILLARD FILLMORE *(left)*
(1800–1874)
President of the United States, 1850–1853
Engraving by Henry B. Hall, Jr.

134

MRS. MILLARD FILLMORE *(right)*
[nee Abigail Powers]
(1798–1853)
First lady, 1850–1853

135

HARVEY SAMUEL FIRESTONE
(left)
(1868–1938)
Rubber manufacturer
Courtesy Firestone Tire and Rubber Co.

136

HAMILTON FISH *(right)*
(1808–1893)
Secretary of State under Grant, U.S. Senator, Governor of New York
Engraving by Alexander H. Ritchie

137

ARTHUR WILLIAM FOOTE *(left)*
(1853–1937)
Composer, organist

138

HENRY FORD *(right)*
(1863–1947)
Automobile manufacturer
Courtesy Automobile Manufacturers Association, Inc.

139
NATHAN BEDFORD FORREST
(*left*)
(1821–1877)
Confederate general
Courtesy Library of Congress

140
STEPHEN COLLINS FOSTER   (*right*)
(1826–1864)
Song writer

141
BENJAMIN FRANKLIN   (*left*)
(1706–1790)
Printer, publisher, statesman, philosopher, inventor
Painting by Joseph Siffred Duplessis. Courtesy Independence National Historical Park

142
MARY WILKINS FREEMAN   (*right*)
[nee Mary Eleanor Wilkins]
(1852–1930)
Short-story writer, novelist

143
JOHN CHARLES FRÉMONT   (*left*)
(1813–1890)
Western explorer, army officer; first Republican presidential candidate (1856)
Engraving by John C. Buttre

144
DANIEL CHESTER FRENCH   (*right*)
(1850–1931)
Sculptor, designed statue for Lincoln Memorial, Washington, D.C.

145

PHILIP MORIN FRENEAU *(left)*
(1752–1832)
Poet, editor, mariner; known as "Poet of the American Revolution"
Engraving by Frederick Halpin

146

HENRY CLAY FRICK *(right)*
(1849–1919)
Steel industrialist, capitalist, art collector; founded Frick Collection, New York

147

BARBARA FRITCHIE *(left)*
[Barbara Frietchie; nee Barbara Hauer]
(1766–1862)
Reputed Civil War heroine, subject of Whittier's poem, "Barbara Frietchie"
After a photograph by Mathew Brady

148

MARGARET FULLER *(right)*
[Marchioness Ossoli, nee Sarah Margaret Fuller]
(1810–1850)
Transcendentalist critic, feminist, journalist

149

ROBERT FULTON *(left)*
(1765–1815)
Engineer, inventor, pioneer in steamboat design, painter
Painting by Charles Willson Peale. Courtesy Independence National Historical Park

150

ALEXANDER GARDNER *(right)*
(1821–1882)
Photographer
Courtesy Acacia Mutual Life Insurance Co.

151
ISABELLA STEWART GARDNER
(*left*)
[nee Isabella Stewart]
(1840–1924)
Boston society leader, art collector; founded
Gardner Museum, Fenway Court
Courtesy Isabella Stewart Gardner Museum

152
JAMES ABRAM GARFIELD   (*right*)
(1831–1881)
President of the United States, 1881
Courtesy National Archives, Brady Collection

153
Mrs. JAMES ABRAM GARFIELD
(*left*)
[nee Lucretia Rudolph]
(1832–1918)
First lady, 1881
Engraving by Samuel Sartain

154
HAMLIN GARLAND   (*right*)
[Hannibal Hamlin Garland]
(1860–1940)
Novelist, short-story writer

155
PAT GARRETT   (*left*)
[Patrick Floyd Garrett]
(1850–1908)
Western lawman, shot Billy the Kid
Courtesy Mercaldo Archives

156
WILLIAM LLOYD GARRISON   (*right*)
(1805–1879)
Abolitionist, lecturer, reformer
Courtesy Library of Congress, Brady-Handy Collection

157
HORATIO GATES   (*left*)
(*c.* 1729–1806)
Revolutionary general
Painting by Gilbert Stuart

158
GERONIMO   (*right*)
[Goyathlay]
(1829–1909)
Apache warrior
Courtesy Mercaldo Archives

159
CHARLES DANA GIBSON   (*left*)
(1867–1944)
Magazine illustrator, creator of the "Gib-son girl"
Courtesy Peter A. Juley & Son

160
CASS GILBERT   (*right*)
(1859–1934)
Architect, designed Woolworth Building, U.S. Supreme Court Building

161
CHARLOTTE GILMAN   (*left*)
[Charlotte Stetson, nee Charlotte Perkins]
(1860–1935)
Writer, lecturer, reformer

162
WILLIAM JAMES GLACKENS   (*right*)
(1870–1938)
Painter, member of the "Ashcan school"
Courtesy Peter A. Juley & Son

163
EMMA GOLDMAN   (*left*)
(1869–1940)
Anarchist, reformer, writer, editor
Courtesy University of Michigan

164
SAMUEL GOMPERS   (*right*)
(1850–1924)
Labor leader; a founder and first president,
American Federation of Labor

165
CHARLES GOODYEAR   (*left*)
(1800–1860)
Inventor, devised process for vulcanizing
rubber
Engraving by W. G. Jackman

166
LOUIS MOREAU GOTTSCHALK
(*right*)
(1829–1869)
Pianist, composer
Courtesy Eric Schaal

167
GEORGE JAY GOULD   (*left*)
(1864–1923)
Railroad industrialist
Photograph by Pach Brothers

168
JAY GOULD   (*right*)
[Jason Gould]
(1836–1892)
Capitalist

169
ULYSSES SIMPSON GRANT *(left)*
(1822–1885)
President of the United States, 1869–1877
Photograph by Alexander Gardner. Courtesy Peter A. Juley & Son

170
MRS. ULYSSES SIMPSON GRANT *(right)*
[nee Julia Dent]
(1826–1902)
First lady, 1869–1877
Courtesy Library of Congress

171
ASA GRAY *(left)*
(1810–1888)
Botanist, writer, educator
Courtesy Library of Congress, Brady-Handy Collection

172
HORACE GREELEY *(right)*
(1811–1872)
Politician; publisher, founder, and editor of the *New York Tribune*

173
NATHANAEL GREENE *(left)*
(1742–1786)
Revolutionary general
Engraved by J. B. Forrest from a painting by John Trumbull

174
SARAH MOORE GRIMKÉ *(right)*
(1792–1873)
Abolitionist, feminist

175
GEORGE BIRD GRINNELL (*left*)
(1849–1938)
Ethnologist, naturalist, writer; edited *Forest and Stream*; influenced founding of Glacier National Park
Courtesy National Park Service, Glacier National Park

176
SOLOMON R. GUGGENHEIM (*right*)
(1861–1949)
Capitalist, donated New York City's Guggenheim Museum
Courtesy Solomon R. Guggenheim Foundation

177
CHARLES J. GUITEAU (*left*)
(c. 1840–1882)
Assassin of President Garfield

178
EDWARD EVERETT HALE (*right*)
(1822–1909)
Writer, editor, Unitarian clergyman, humanitarian

179
SARAH HALE (*left*)
[nee Sarah Josepha Buell]
(1788–1879)
Writer, reformer; edited *Ladies' Magazine* and *Godey's Lady's Book*
Engraving by John C. Buttre

180
ALEXANDER HAMILTON (*right*)
(1757–1804)
First U.S. Secretary of the Treasury (1789–1795); signer of Constitution, principal author of *The Federalist*
Engraved by J. F. E. Prud'homme from a painting by Archibald Robertson

181
HANNIBAL HAMLIN   (*left*)
(1809–1891)
Congressman, U.S. Senator, Governor of Maine; Vice-President of U.S., 1861–1865

182
JOHN HANCOCK   (*right*)
(1737–1793)
Signer of Declaration of Independence; president of Continental Congress; first governor of Massachusetts
Painting by John Singleton Copley

183
WINFIELD SCOTT HANCOCK   (*left*)
(1824–1886)
Union general in Civil War, presidential candidate
Engraving by Robert Whitechurch

184
WARREN GAMALIEL HARDING
(*right*)
(1865–1923)
President of the United States, 1921–1923
Courtesy Library of Congress

185
Mrs. WARREN G. HARDING   (*left*)
[nee Florence Kling]
(1860–1924)
First lady, 1921–1923
Courtesy Harding Home and Museum

186
JOEL CHANDLER HARRIS   (*right*)
(1848–1908)
Journalist, writer; author of "Uncle Remus" tales

Harris   31

187
BENJAMIN HARRISON *(left)*
(c. 1726–1791)
Governor of Virginia; member of Continental Congress; signer of Declaration of Independence
Painted by James Reid Lambdin from a painting by John Trumbull. Courtesy Independence National Historical Park

188
BENJAMIN HARRISON *(right)*
(1833–1901)
President of the United States, 1889–1893
Courtesy Benjamin H. Walker

189
Mrs. BENJAMIN HARRISON *(left)*
[nee Caroline Lavinia Scott]
(1832–1892)
First lady, 1889–1892

190
WILLIAM HENRY HARRISON
(right)
(1773–1841)
President of the United States, 1841
Photograph by Southworth and Hawes. Courtesy Metropolitan Museum of Art, Stokes-Hawes Collection

191
Mrs. WILLIAM HENRY HARRISON
(left)
[nee Anna Symmes]
(1775–1864)
First lady, 1841

192
WILLIAM S. HART *(right)*
(1872–1946)
Actor
Courtesy Newhall-Saugus Chamber of Commerce

193
BRET HARTE (*left*)
[Francis Brett Harte]
(1836–1902)
Short-story writer, novelist, poet

194
CHILDE HASSAM   (*right*)
[Frederick Childe Hassam]
(1859–1935)
Painter, etcher
Courtesy Peter A. Juley & Son

195
NATHANIEL HAWTHORNE (*left*)
(1804–1864)
Novelist, short-story writer
Courtesy National Archives, Brady Collection

196
RUTHERFORD BIRCHARD HAYES
(*right*)
(1822–1893)
President of the United States, 1877–1881
Courtesy Library of Congress, Brady-Handy Collection

197
Mrs. RUTHERFORD B. HAYES
(*left*)
[nee Lucy Ware Webb]
(1831–1889)
First lady, 1877–1881
Engraving by John Sartain

198
LAFCADIO HEARN (*right*)
[Patricio Lafcadio Tessima Carlos Hearn]
(1850–1904)
Journalist, translator, novelist, student of
Japanese culture

199
WILLIAM RANDOLPH HEARST
(*left*)
(1863–1951)
Newspaper publisher, capitalist
Courtesy William Randolph Hearst, Jr.

200
ROBERT HENRI   (*right*)
(1865–1929)
Painter, one of "The Eight"
Courtesy Peter A. Juley & Son

201
O. HENRY   (*left*)
[William Sydney Porter]
(1862–1910)
Short-story writer

202
PATRICK HENRY   (*right*)
(1736–1799)
Revolutionary leader, member of Continental Congress, Governor of Virginia
Painting by Thomas Sully. Courtesy Colonial Williamsburg

203
JOSIAH HENSON   (*left*)
(1789–1883)
Escaped slave, Methodist preacher; reputed model for Uncle Tom in *Uncle Tom's Cabin*

204
MATTHEW HENSON   (*right*)
(1866–1955)
Explorer, member of Peary expedition to North Pole

205
VICTOR HERBERT   *(left)*
(1859–1924)
Operetta composer

206
WILD BILL HICKOK   *(right)*
[James Butler Hickok]
(1837–1876)
Law officer, U.S. marshal in the West
Courtesy Mercaldo Archives

207
EDWARD HICKS   *(left)*
(1780–1849)
Painter
Painting by Thomas Hicks

208
THOMAS WENTWORTH
HIGGINSON   *(right)*
[Thomas Wentworth Storrow Higginson]
(1823–1911)
Writer, biographer; Unitarian clergyman,
abolitionist, reformer
Engraving by Charles B. Hall

209
DOC HOLLIDAY   *(left)*
[Dr. John H. Holliday]
(1850–1885)
Western gunman, aided Wyatt Earp in
battle of O.K. Corral
Courtesy Mercaldo Archives

210
OLIVER WENDELL HOLMES   *(right)*
(1809–1894)
Poet, essayist, novelist, physician, educator

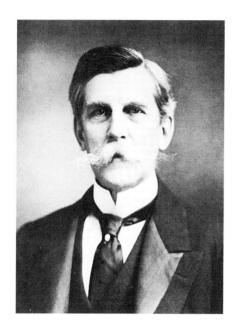

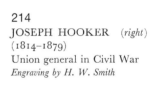

217
HARRY HOUDINI   *(left)*
[Ehrich Weiss]
(1874–1926)
Magician, writer

218
SAMUEL HOUSTON   *(right)*
(1793–1863)
Leader of Texas independence; first president, Texas Republic; U.S. Senator, Governor of Texas
Painting by Edward Schnabel. Courtesy Gregory's Old Master Gallery

219
ELIAS HOWE   *(left)*
(1819–1867)
Inventor of the sewing machine
Photograph by Southworth and Hawes. Courtesy Metropolitan Museum of Art, Stokes-Hawes Collection

220
JULIA WARD HOWE   *(right)*
[nee Julia Ward]
(1819–1910)
Abolitionist, reformer, writer; author of "The Battle Hymn of the Republic"

221
WILLIAM DEAN HOWELLS   *(left)*
(1837–1920)
Novelist, critic, editor of *The Atlantic Monthly*

222
GEORGE INNESS   *(right)*
(1825–1894)
Landscape painter
Courtesy Peter A. Juley & Son

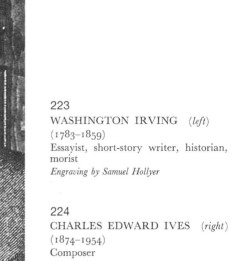

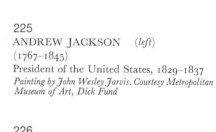

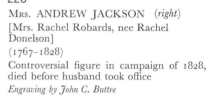

223
WASHINGTON IRVING (left)
(1783–1859)
Essayist, short-story writer, historian, humorist
Engraving by Samuel Hollyer

224
CHARLES EDWARD IVES (right)
(1874–1954)
Composer

225
ANDREW JACKSON (left)
(1767–1845)
President of the United States, 1829–1837
Painting by John Wesley Jarvis. Courtesy Metropolitan Museum of Art, Dick Fund

226
MRS. ANDREW JACKSON (right)
[Mrs. Rachel Robards, nee Rachel Donelson]
(1767–1828)
Controversial figure in campaign of 1828, died before husband took office
Engraving by John C. Buttre

227
HELEN HUNT JACKSON (left)
[nee Helen Maria Fiske]
(1830–1885)
Novelist, poet, journalist, reformer

228
STONEWALL JACKSON (right)
[Thomas Jonathan Jackson]
(1824–1863)
Confederate general

229
FRANK JAMES (left)
[Alexander Franklin James]
(c. 1844–1915)
Western outlaw
Courtesy Mercaldo Archives

230
HENRY JAMES (right)
(1843–1916)
Novelist, short-story writer, critic

231
JESSE JAMES (left)
[Jesse Woodson James]
(1847–1882)
Western outlaw
Courtesy Mercaldo Archives

232
WILLIAM JAMES (right)
(1842–1910)
Philosopher, psychologist

233
JOHN JAY (left)
(1745–1829)
Diplomat, statesman; co-author, *The Federalist*; first Chief Justice of U.S., 1790–1795
Painting by Gilbert Stuart

234
THOMAS JEFFERSON (right)
(1743–1826)
President of the United States, 1801–1809
Painting attributed to James Sharples, Sr. Courtesy Independence National Historical Park

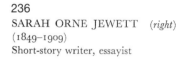

235
JAMES J. JEFFRIES *(left)*
(1875–1953)
Heavyweight boxing champion
Courtesy Mercaldo Archives

236
SARAH ORNE JEWETT *(right)*
(1849–1909)
Short-story writer, essayist

237
ANDREW JOHNSON *(left)*
(1808–1875)
President of the United States, 1865–1869
Engraving by Alexander H. Ritchie

238
Mrs. ANDREW JOHNSON *(right)*
[nee Eliza McCardle]
(1810–1876)
First lady, 1865–1869
Engraving by John C. Buttre

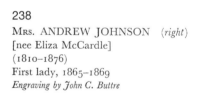

239
CASEY JONES *(left)*
[John Luther Jones]
(1864–1900)
Railroad engineer aboard the "Cannonball
Express"
Courtesy Illinois Central Railroad

240
JOHN PAUL JONES *(right)*
[John Paul]
(1747–1792)
Naval officer in Revolutionary War
Painting by Charles Willson Peale. Courtesy Independence National Historical Park

241
MARY JONES   *(left)*
["Mother Jones," nee Mary Harris]
(1830–1930)
Labor agitator and organizer
Courtesy Tamiment Institute Library

242
CHIEF JOSEPH   *(right)*
[Hinmaton-Yalaktit]
(c. 1840–1904)
Nez Percé Indian chief

243
THEODORE DEHONE JUDAH
(left)
(1826–1863)
Railroad financier, promoted construction of
Central Pacific Railroad
Courtesy California Historical Society

244
Mme STEPHEN JUMEL   *(right)*
[nee Eliza Brown; Betsey Bowen]
(1769–1865)
Controversial New York society figure; later
married Aaron Burr
Courtesy Jumel Mansion

245
ELISHA KENT KANE   *(left)*
(1820–1857)
Arctic explorer, physician
*Engraved by Thomas Phillibrowne from a photograph
by Mathew Brady*

246
PHILIP KEARNY   *(right)*
(1814–1862)
Union general in Civil War
Engraving by John C. Buttre

247
STEPHEN WATTS KEARNY *(left)*
(1794–1848)
Army officer in Mexican War
Engraving by Thomas B. Welch

248
HELEN ADAMS KELLER *(right)*
(1880–1968)
Blind and deaf writer and lecturer

249
FRANK BILLINGS KELLOGG *(left)*
(1856–1937)
U.S. Senator, diplomat, Secretary of State
under Coolidge; Nobel Peace Laureate
Courtesy Library of Congress

250
FRANCIS SCOTT KEY *(right)*
(1779–1843)
Lawyer, author of "The Star-Spangled
Banner"

251
THADDEUS KOSCIUSKO *(left)*
[Tadeusz Andrzej Bonawentura Kościuszko]
(1746–1817)
Polish patriot, general in Continental Army

252
JOHN La FARGE *(right)*
(1835–1910)
Painter, muralist, designed stained-glass
windows
Courtesy Peter A. Juley & Son

253
JOHN BAPTIST LAMY (*left*)
[Jean Baptiste l'Amy]
(1814–1888)
Roman Catholic prelate, model for Willa
Cather's *Death Comes for the Archbishop*

254
SIDNEY LANIER (*right*)
(1842–1881)
Poet, musician, critic
Engraving by H. B. Hall's Sons

255
LUCY LARCOM (*left*)
(1824–1893)
Writer, editor, teacher

256
BENJAMIN HENRY LATROBE (*right*)
(1764–1820)
Architect, engineer; supervised reconstruc-
tion of U.S. Capitol following War of 1812
Painting by Charles Willson Peale

257
EMMA LAZARUS (*left*)
(1849–1887)
Poet, essayist, author of Statue of Liberty
sonnet

258
HENRY LEE (*right*)
[Light-Horse Harry Lee]
(1756–1818)
Revolutionary cavalry commander, legislator; suppressed Whisky Rebellion; eulo-
gized Washington as "first in war, first in
peace . . ."
*Painting by Charles Willson Peale. Courtesy Inde-
pendence National Historical Park*

259
RICHARD HENRY LEE   *(left)*
(1732–1794)
Revolutionary patriot, legislator; signer of Declaration of Independence
Painting by Charles Willson Peale. Courtesy Independence National Historical Park

260
ROBERT EDWARD LEE   *(right)*
(1807–1870)
Commander, Confederate armies
Courtesy Library of Congress, Brady-Handy Collection

261
MERIWETHER LEWIS   *(left)*
(1774–1809)
Explored American Northwest with William Clark
Painting by Charles Willson Peale

262
ABRAHAM LINCOLN   *(right)*
(1809–1865)
President of the United States, 1861–1865
Engraving by H. B. Hall's Sons

263
MRS. ABRAHAM LINCOLN   *(left)*
[nee Mary Todd]
(1818–1882)
First lady, 1861–1865
Courtesy New-York Historical Society

264
JENNY LIND   *(right)*
[Mme Jennie Lind-Goldschmidt; nee Johanna Maria Lind]
(1820–1887)
Coloratura soprano, "the Swedish Nightingale"; toured U.S. with Barnum
Courtesy New-York Historical Society

265
HENRY DEMAREST LLOYD (*left*)
(1847–1903)
Journalist, writer, Socialist; first of the muckrakers

266
JACK LONDON (*right*)
[John Griffith London]
(1876–1916)
Novelist, short-story writer
Courtesy Library of Congress

267
HENRY WADSWORTH
LONGFELLOW (*left*)
(1807–1882)
Poet, translator
Engraving by H. B. Hall & Sons

268
JAMES LONGSTREET (*right*)
(1821–1904)
Confederate general

269
JAMES RUSSELL LOWELL (*left*)
(1819–1891)
Poet, essayist, educator, diplomat

270
GEORGE BRINTON McCLELLAN
(*right*)
(1826–1885)
Union general in Civil War
Courtesy New-York Historical Society

271
CYRUS HALL McCORMICK   (left)
(1809–1884)
Inventor, manufacturer; invented the reaper

272
EDWARD ALEXANDER
MacDOWELL   (right)
(1861–1908)
Composer, pianist
Courtesy Library of Congress

273
WILLIAM McKINLEY   (left)
(1843–1901)
President of the United States, 1897–1901

274
Mrs. WILLIAM McKINLEY   (right)
[nee Ida Saxton]
(1847–1907)
First lady, 1897–1901

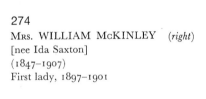

275
DOLLY MADISON   (left)
[Dolley Madison; Mrs. James Madison, nee
Dorothea Payne]
(1768–1849)
Washington social leader; first lady, 1809–
1817
Painting by Gilbert Stuart

276
JAMES MADISON   (right)
(1751–1836)
President of the United States, 1809–1817
Painting by Gilbert Stuart

277
ALFRED THAYER MAHAN (*left*)
(1840–1914)
Naval officer, historian, strategist
Courtesy U.S. Department of Defense

278
FRANCIS MARION (*right*)
(*c.* 1732–1795)
Revolutionary commander; "The Swamp Fox"

279
JOHN MARSHALL (*left*)
(1755–1835)
Chief Justice of U.S., 1801–1835; diplomat, Congressman, Secretary of State under John Adams
Painting by Rembrandt Peale. Courtesy Virginia Museum of Fine Arts, The Glasgow Fund

280
HARRIET MARTINEAU (*right*)
(1802–1876)
English novelist, economist; wrote on life in U.S.
After a painting by Alonzo Chappel

281
GEORGE MASON (*left*)
(1725–1792)
Revolutionary leader, author of Virginia Declaration of Rights, delegate to Constitutional Convention
After a painting by John Hesselius. Courtesy Independence National Historical Park

282
EDGAR LEE MASTERS (*right*)
(1869–1950)
Poet
Courtesy American Academy of Arts and Letters

Masters 47

283
BAT MASTERSON (left)
[William Barclay Masterson]
(1853–1921)
Frontier marshal, gambler; sports writer for
New York Morning Telegraph
Courtesy Mercaldo Archives

284
COTTON MATHER (right)
(1663–1728)
Congregational clergyman, Puritan zealot,
writer; investigated witchcraft
Painting by Peter Pelham

285
INCREASE MATHER (left)
(1639–1723)
Congregational clergyman, Massachusetts
colony leader; president of Harvard College
Painting by Jan Van Der Spriett

286
RICHARD MATHER (right)
(1596–1669)
Congregational clergyman, early leader of
Massachusetts colony
Woodcut by John Foster

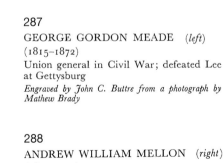

287
GEORGE GORDON MEADE (left)
(1815–1872)
Union general in Civil War; defeated Lee
at Gettysburg
*Engraved by John C. Buttre from a photograph by
Mathew Brady*

288
ANDREW WILLIAM MELLON (right)
(1855–1937)
Financier, diplomat; Secretary of the
Treasury under Harding, Coolidge, and
Hoover; founder, National Gallery of Art
*Painting by Oswald Birley. Courtesy National Gallery
of Art. Gift of Ailsa Mellon Bruce*

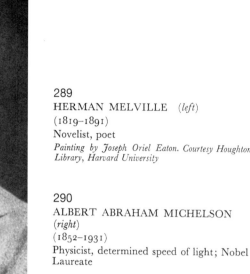

289
HERMAN MELVILLE *(left)*
(1819–1891)
Novelist, poet
Painting by Joseph Oriel Eaton. Courtesy Houghton Library, Harvard University

290
ALBERT ABRAHAM MICHELSON
(right)
(1852–1931)
Physicist, determined speed of light; Nobel Laureate

291
JAMES MONROE *(left)*
(1758–1831)
President of the United States, 1817–1825
Painting by Gilbert Stuart

292
Mrs. JAMES MONROE *(right)*
[nee Eliza Kortright; Elizabeth Kortright]
(1768–1830)
First lady, 1817–1825
After a miniature by Sené

293
LOLA MONTEZ *(left)*
[Marie Dolores Eliza Rosanna Gilbert]
(c. 1818–1861)
English adventuress, dancer; settled in U.S.
Photograph by Southworth and Hawes. Courtesy Metropolitan Museum of Art, Stokes-Hawes Collection

294
CLEMENT CLARKE MOORE *(right)*
(1779–1863)
Hebraic scholar, poet; wrote "'Twas the night before Christmas . . ."

295
DANIEL MORGAN   (left)
(1736–1802)
Revolutionary general, suppressed Whisky
Rebellion
Painting by Charles Willson Peale. Courtesy Independence National Historical Park

296
J. P. MORGAN   (right)
[John Pierpont Morgan]
(1837–1913)
Financier, art collector
Courtesy Library of Congress

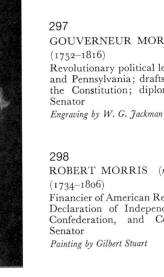

297
GOUVERNEUR MORRIS   (left)
(1752–1816)
Revolutionary political leader in New York
and Pennsylvania; draftsman and signer of
the Constitution; diplomat, diarist, U.S.
Senator
Engraving by W. G. Jackman

298
ROBERT MORRIS   (right)
(1734–1806)
Financier of American Revolution; signer of
Declaration of Independence, Articles of
Confederation, and Constitution; U.S.
Senator
Painting by Gilbert Stuart

299
SAMUEL FINLEY BREESE MORSE
(left)
(1791–1872)
Inventor of electric telegraph and Morse
code; painter; first president, National
Academy of Design

300
JOHN SINGLETON MOSBY   (right)
(1833–1916)
Confederate ranger, lawyer
Courtesy Library of Congress, Brady-Handy Collection

301
LUCRETIA MOTT   (*left*)
[nee Lucretia Coffin]
(1793–1880)
Quaker preacher, abolitionist, feminist
Engraving by George E. Perine

302
JOHN MUIR   (*right*)
(1838–1914)
Naturalist, conservationist, writer
Courtesy Sierra Club

303
EADWEARD MUYBRIDGE   (*left*)
[Edward James Muggeridge]
(1830–1904)
Pioneer in photography of motion

304
THOMAS NAST   (*right*)
(1840–1902)
Political cartoonist, attacked Tweed Ring

305
NATCHEZ   (*left*)
(*born, c.* 1858)
Apache Indian, son of Cochise; ally of
Geronimo

306
CARRY NATION   (*right*)
[nee Carry Amelia Moore]
(1846–1911)
Temperance agitator, social reformer
Courtesy Kansas State Historical Society

307
FRANK NORRIS (left)
[Benjamin Franklin Norris, Jr.]
(1870–1902)
Novelist, author of *McTeague*
Courtesy Doubleday & Co.

308
ANNIE OAKLEY (right)
[Phoebe Anne Oakley Mozee]
(1860–1926)
Marksman, circus performer
Courtesy Mercaldo Archives

309
FREDERICK LAW OLMSTED (left)
(1822–1903)
Landscape architect; designed Central
Park, New York, and Prospect Park, Brook-
lyn

310
JAMES OTIS (right)
(1725–1783)
Revolutionary agitator, politician, political
writer
*Engraved by W. G. Jackman after a painting by John
Singleton Copley*

311
ROBERT OWEN (left)
(1771–1858)
Welsh socialist; founded utopian society at
New Harmony, Indiana
*Courtesy Don Blair, New Harmony Workingmen's
Institute*

312
THOMAS PAINE (right)
(1737–1809)
Revolutionary agitator, pamphleteer, phi-
losopher; author of *The Age of Reason*
*Engraved by Illman & Sons after a painting by George
Romney*

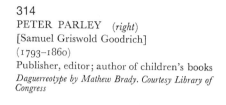

313
FRANCIS PARKMAN   (*left*)
(1823–1893)
Historian
Engraving by H. B. Hall's Sons

314
PETER PARLEY   (*right*)
[Samuel Griswold Goodrich]
(1793–1860)
Publisher, editor; author of children's books
Daguerreotype by Mathew Brady. Courtesy Library of Congress

315
GEORGE PEABODY   (*left*)
(1795–1869)
Merchant, financier, philanthropist; endowed Peabody Institute, Baltimore

316
CHARLES WILLSON PEALE   (*right*)
(1741–1827)
Portrait painter, naturalist
Self-portrait. Courtesy Pennsylvania Academy of the Fine Arts

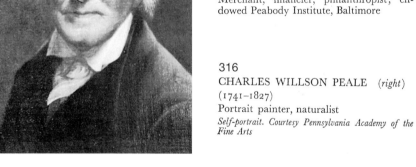

317
WILLIAM PENN   (*left*)
(1644–1718)
English Quaker leader, proprietor of Pennsylvania
Engraved by John Sartain from a painting attributed to Sir Peter Lely

318
JOSEPH PENNELL   (*right*)
(1857–1926)
Graphic artist, writer
Photograph by Pirie MacDonald. Courtesy New-York Historical Society

Pennell   53

319
MATTHEW CALBRAITH PERRY
(*left*)
(1794–1858)
Naval officer, opened Japan to West
Courtesy New-York Historical Society

320
JOHN JOSEPH PERSHING   (*right*)
["Black Jack" Pershing]
(1860–1948)
General, army chief of staff; command-
ed American Expeditionary Force, World
War I
Courtesy Library of Congress

321
DUNCAN PHYFE   (*left*)
(1768–1854)
Furniture maker

322
GEORGE EDWARD PICKETT   (*right*)
(1825–1875)
Confederate general; repulsed in decisive
charge at Gettysburg
Courtesy Library of Congress, Brady Collection

323
FRANKLIN PIERCE   (*left*)
(1804–1869)
President of the United States, 1853–1857

324
MRS. FRANKLIN PIERCE   (*right*)
[nee Jane Means Appleton]
(1806–1863)
First lady, 1853–1857
Engraving by John C. Buttre. Courtesy Library of Congress

325
ZEBULON MONTGOMERY PIKE
(left)
(1779–1813)
Army officer, Western explorer; discovered
Pikes Peak
Painting by Charles Willson Peale. Courtesy Independence National Historical Park

326
POCAHONTAS   (right)
[Matoaka]
(c. 1595–1617)
Indian maiden, daughter of Powhatan; said
to have saved John Smith; married John
Rolfe

327
EDGAR ALLAN POE   (left)
(1809–1849)
Poet, critic, short-story writer
Courtesy National Archives, Brady Collection

328
JAMES KNOX POLK   (right)
(1795–1849)
President of the United States, 1845–1849
Painting by G. P. A. Healy

329
Mrs. JAMES KNOX POLK   (left)
[nee Sarah Childress]
(1803–1891)
First lady, 1845–1849

330
MAURICE BRAZIL PRENDERGAST
(right)
(1861–1924)
Painter
Courtesy Oliver Baker Associates

331
CASIMIR PULASKI (*left*)
(*c.* 1748–1779)
Polish officer in American Revolution; mortally wounded in siege of Savannah

332
JOSEPH PULITZER (*right*)
(1847–1911)
Newspaper publisher; founded school of journalism, Columbia University
Painting by John Singer Sargent. Courtesy Columbiana Collection, Columbia University

333
GEORGE HAVEN PUTNAM (*left*)
(1844–1930)
Publisher, writer, civic leader; advocate of copyright reform

334
HOWARD PYLE (*right*)
(1853–1911)
Illustrator, writer, teacher
Courtesy Peter A. Juley & Son

335
WILLIAM CLARKE QUANTRILL
(*left*)
(1837–1865)
Confederate guerrilla commander; led raid on Lawrence, Kansas
Courtesy Smithsonian Institution

336
CONSTANTINE SAMUEL
RAFINESQUE (*right*)
[Constantine Samuel Rafinesque-Schmaltz]
(1783–1840)
Botanist, ichthyologist, writer

337
RAIN-IN-THE-FACE   *(left)*
(c. 1843–1905)
Sioux Indian chief, leader at battle of Little
Big Horn
Courtesy Mercaldo Archives

338
RED CLOUD   *(right)*
(1822–1909)
Oglala Indian chief
Courtesy Mercaldo Archives

339
FREDERIC REMINGTON   *(left)*
(1861–1909)
Painter, sculptor, illustrator, writer

340
PAUL REVERE   *(right)*
(1735–1818)
Revolutionary patriot, silversmith, engraver
Painting by Gilbert Stuart

341
JACOB AUGUST RIIS   *(left)*
(1849–1914)
Journalist, writer, photographer; exposed
slum conditions in New York City
Courtesy Library of Congress

342
JAMES WHITCOMB RILEY   *(right)*
(1849–1916)
Hoosier poet

Riley   57

343
EDWIN ARLINGTON ROBINSON
(*left*)
(1869–1935)
Poet
*Photograph by Pirie MacDonald. Courtesy American
Academy of Arts and Letters*

344
JOHN AUGUSTUS ROEBLING (*right*)
(1806–1869)
Civil engineer, designed Brooklyn Bridge

345
WASHINGTON AUGUSTUS
ROEBLING (*left*)
(1837–1926)
Civil engineer, supervised construction of
Brooklyn Bridge
Courtesy John A. Roebling's Sons Corporation

346
ELEANOR ROOSEVELT (*right*)
[Anna Eleanor Roosevelt]
(1884–1962)
First lady, 1933–1945; humanitarian
Courtesy Library of Congress

347
FRANKLIN DELANO ROOSEVELT
(*left*)
(1882–1945)
President of the United States, 1933–1945
*Painting by Frank O. Salisbury. Courtesy Franklin D.
Roosevelt Library*

348
THEODORE ROOSEVELT (*right*)
(1858–1919)
President of the United States, 1901–1909

349
MRS. THEODORE ROOSEVELT (*left*)
[nee Edith Kermit Carow]
(1861–1948)
First lady, 1901–1909

350
JOSIAH ROYCE (*right*)
(1855–1916)
Philosopher, writer, educator

351
BENJAMIN RUSH (*left*)
(*c.* 1745–1813)
Physician, chemist, natural philosopher; signer of Declaration of Independence
Engraved by Richard W. Dodson after a painting by Thomas Sully

352
LILLIAN RUSSELL (*right*)
[Helen Louise Leonard]
(1861–1922)
Actress, singer; starred in comic-opera roles
Photograph by Napoleon Sarony

353
AUGUSTUS SAINT-GAUDENS (*left*)
(1848–1907)
Sculptor

354
GEORGE SANTAYANA (*right*)
(1863–1952)
Philosopher, poet, novelist, educator

Santayana 59

355
JOHN SINGER SARGENT   (left)
(1856–1925)
Painter
Courtesy Peter A. Juley & Son

356
HENRY ROWE SCHOOLCRAFT
(right)
(1793–1864)
Ethnologist, geologist, explorer; studied American Indians
Engraving by Wellstood and Peters

357
DRED SCOTT   (left)
(c. 1795–1858)
Negro slave, denied freedom by Supreme Court in *Dred Scott v. Sanford*
Courtesy New-York Historical Society

358
WINFIELD SCOTT   (right)
(1786–1866)
General-in-chief, U.S. Army, 1841–1861
Photograph by Mathew Brady

359
Mother ELIZABETH SETON   (left)
[nee Elizabeth Ann Bayley]
(1774–1821)
Leader of Catholic charitable and educational work; beatified 1963
Courtesy Mount St. Vincent-on-Hudson

360
SAMUEL SEWALL   (right)
(1652–1730)
Colonial jurist; judge at Salem witchcraft trials
After a painting attributed to John Smibert

361
WILLIAM HENRY SEWARD (*left*)
(1801–1872)
Secretary of State under Lincoln and
Andrew Johnson, U.S. Senator; negotiated
purchase of Alaska
*Retouched photograph by Mathew Brady. Courtesy
U.S. Department of State*

362
ROBERT GOULD SHAW (*right*)
(1837–1863)
Union officer, commanded first free-state
Negro regiment in Civil War

363
PHILIP HENRY SHERIDAN (*left*)
(1831–1888)
Union general in Civil War
Courtesy New-York Historical Society

364
ROGER SHERMAN (*right*)
(1721–1793)
Connecticut legislator; only man to sign
Declaration of Independence, Articles of
Association, Articles of Confederation, and
the Constitution
*Engraved by Simeon S. Jocelyn from a painting by
Ralph Earle*

365
WILLIAM TECUMSEH SHERMAN
(*left*)
[Tecumseh Sherman]
(1820–1891)
Union general in Civil War, devastated
Georgia on march to sea
Courtesy New-York Historical Society

366
SITTING BULL (*right*)
(c. 1834–1890)
Sioux Indian chief
Courtesy Mercaldo Archives

367
JOHN SLOAN   (*left*)
(1871–1951)
Painter, etcher
Courtesy Peter A. Juley & Son

368
JOSHUA SLOCUM   (*right*)
(1844–*c*.1910)
Sailor, adventurer, writer; sailed alone around the world

369
JOSEPH SMITH   (*left*)
(1805–1844)
Prophet and founder of the Mormon Church
Courtesy Church of Jesus Christ of Latter-Day Saints

370
JOHN PHILIP SOUSA   (*right*)
(1854–1932)
Bandmaster, composer of marches

371
MYLES STANDISH   (*left*)
(*c.* 1584–1656)
Pilgrim leader

372
Sir HENRY MORTON STANLEY (*right*)
[John Rowlands]
(1841–1904)
Journalist, African explorer, found David Livingstone

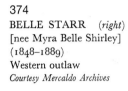

373
ELIZABETH STANTON   (*left*)
[nee Elizabeth Cady]
(1815–1902)
Reformer, advocate of women's rights
Courtesy Tamiment Institute Library

374
BELLE STARR   (*right*)
[nee Myra Belle Shirley]
(1848–1889)
Western outlaw
Courtesy Mercaldo Archives

375
LINCOLN STEFFENS   (*left*)
[Joseph Lincoln Steffens]
(1866–1936)
Journalist, reformer, editor; exposed political corruption of large cities
Photograph by Pirie MacDonald. Courtesy New-York Historical Society

376
ALFRED STIEGLITZ   (*right*)
(1864–1946)
Photographer, editor, art patron
Courtesy Georgia O'Keeffe

377
JOSEPH STORY   (*left*)
(1779–1845)
Associate justice, U.S. Supreme Court; legal scholar, a founder of Harvard Law School
Engraved by J. Cheney after a drawing by William Wetmore Story

378
HARRIET BEECHER STOWE   (*right*)
[nee Harriet Elizabeth Beecher]
(1811–1896)
Novelist, abolitionist, wrote *Uncle Tom's Cabin*

379
LEVI STRAUSS (*left*)
(*c.* 1828–1903)
Clothing manufacturer—"Levi's"
Courtesy Levi Strauss & Co.

380
GEORGE TEMPLETON STRONG
(*right*)
(1820–1875)
Diarist, described mid-nineteenth century
life in New York

381
GILBERT STUART (*left*)
[Gilbert Charles Stuart]
(1755–1828)
Painter
Self-portrait

382
JEB STUART (*right*)
[James Ewell Brown Stuart]
(1833–1864)
Confederate general, cavalry commander
Engraving by Alexander H. Ritchie

383
PETER STUYVESANT (*left*)
[Petrus Stuyvesant]
(1592–1672)
Dutch director-general of New Netherland
Engraving by Charles Burt

384
ANNE SULLIVAN (*right*)
[Mrs. Anne Mansfield Macy]
(1866–1936)
Educator of the blind; teacher and friend of
Helen Keller
Courtesy American Foundation for the Blind, Inc.

385
JOHN L. SULLIVAN (*left*)
[John Lawrence Sullivan]
(1858–1918)
Prize fighter, last bare-knuckle heavyweight champion
Courtesy Mercaldo Archives

386
LOUIS HENRI SULLIVAN (*right*)
(1856–1924)
Chicago architect, advocated functional treatment of skyscraper

387
THOMAS SULLY (*left*)
(1783–1872)
Portrait painter
Engraved by John Sartain from a self-portrait

388
CHARLES SUMNER (*right*)
(1811–1874)
Abolitionist, U.S. Senator, Reconstruction leader; assaulted in Senate chamber
Engraving by George E. Perine

389
MARY E. SURRATT (*left*)
(1820–1865)
Alleged member of Booth conspiracy, hanged after Lincoln's assassination
Courtesy New-York Historical Society

390
JOHN AUGUSTUS SUTTER (*right*)
[Johan August Suter]
(1803–1880)
California settler, owned site of first gold discovery, 1848
Painting by Samuel A. Osgood. Courtesy New-York Historical Society

391
WILLIAM HOWARD TAFT   (*left*)
(1857–1930)
President of the United States, 1909–1913;
Chief Justice of the United States, 1921–
1930
Courtesy Library of Congress

392
Mrs. WILLIAM HOWARD TAFT
(*right*)
[nee Helen Herron]
(1861–1943)
First lady, 1909–1913

393
BENJAMIN TALLMADGE   (*left*)
(1754–1835)
Revolutionary officer, Congressman
Engraved by George Parker from a painting by Ezra Ames

394
ROGER BROOKE TANEY   (*right*)
(1777–1864)
Chief Justice of U.S., 1836–1864; Attorney General and Secretary of the Treasury under Jackson
Courtesy Library of Congress

395
IDA MINERVA TARBELL   (*left*)
(1857–1944)
Reformer, writer; early muckraker

396
BOOTH TARKINGTON   (*right*)
[Newton Booth Tarkington]
(1869–1946)
Novelist

397
BAYARD TAYLOR   (*left*)
[James Bayard Taylor]
(1825–1878)
Traveler, travel writer, translator, poet

398
ZACHARY TAYLOR   (*right*)
(1784–1850)
President of the United States, 1849–1850
Engraving by Alexander H. Ritchie

399
MRS. ZACHARY TAYLOR   (*left*)
[nee Margaret Mackall Smith]
(1787–1852)
First lady, 1849–1850

400
TECUMSEH   (*right*)
[Tikamthi; Tecumtha]
(1768–1813)
Shawnee Indian chief
Courtesy Bureau of American Ethnology, Smithsonian Institution

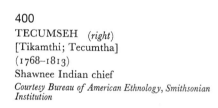

401
SYLVANUS THAYER   (*left*)
(1785–1872)
Engineer; superintendent of West Point; "Father of the Military Academy"
Painting by Julian Alden Weir. U. S. Army Photograph, courtesy U. S. Military Academy

402
GENERAL TOM THUMB   (*right*)
[Charles Sherwood Stratton]
(1838–1883)
Barnum's famed midget
Courtesy New-York Historical Society

Tom Thumb   67

403

MRS. TOM THUMB *(left)*

[Mrs. Charles Sherwood Stratton; Lavinia Warren, nee Mercy Lavinia Warren Bumpus]

(1841–1919)

Barnum midget, wife of General Tom Thumb

Courtesy Museum of the City of New York

404

LOUIS COMFORT TIFFANY *(right)*

(1848–1933)

Designer and manufacturer of colored-glass products, "Tiffany glass"

Courtesy Tiffany & Co.

405

HENRY TIMROD *(left)*

(1828–1867)

"Poet laureate of the Confederacy"

Courtesy South Caroliniana Library, University of South Carolina

406

HARRY S. TRUMAN *(right)*

(1884–1972)

President of the United States, 1945–1953

Courtesy Harry S. Truman Library

407

MRS. HARRY S. TRUMAN *(left)*

[Bess Truman, nee Elizabeth Virginia Wallace]

(1885–1982)

First lady, 1945–1953

Courtesy Harry S. Truman Library

408

JOHN TRUMBULL *(right)*

(1756–1843)

Painter of portraits, Revolutionary War scenes

Engraved by Asher B. Durand from a painting by Waldo & Jewett

409
HARRIET TUBMAN *(left)*
[nee Harriet Ross]
(*c.* 1821–1913)
Escaped slave, abolitionist, Negro leader
Courtesy Library of Congress

410
FREDERICK JACKSON TURNER
(right)
(1861–1932)
Historian, educator; originated frontier interpretation of American history
Courtesy University of Wisconsin

411
MARK TWAIN *(left)*
[Samuel Langhorne Clemens]
(1835–1910)
Novelist, humorist, lecturer

412
WILLIAM MARCY TWEED *(right)*
[Boss Tweed]
(1823–1878)
Politician, Congressman; leader of Tammany Hall, New York
After a photograph by Mathew Brady

413
JOHN TYLER *(left)*
(1790–1862)
President of the United States, 1841–1845
Engraving by Henry B. Hall, Jr.

414
Mrs. JOHN TYLER *(right)*
[nee Letitia Christian]
(1790–1842)
First lady, 1841–1842
Engraving by J. C. Buttre

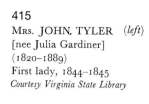

415
MRS. JOHN. TYLER   (*left*)
[nee Julia Gardiner]
(1820–1889)
First lady, 1844–1845
Courtesy Virginia State Library

416
ANGELICA VAN BUREN   (*right*)
[Mrs. Abram Van Buren, nee Angelica
Singleton]
(1816–1878)
Daughter-in-law of Martin Van Buren;
White House hostess
Engraving by J. C. Buttre

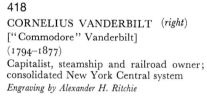
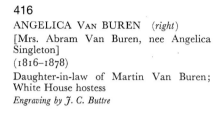

417
MARTIN VAN BUREN   (*left*)
(1782–1862)
President of the United States, 1837–1841
*Painted by Eliphalet Fraser Andrews after a painting
by G. P. A. Healy. Courtesy U.S. Department of State*

418
CORNELIUS VANDERBILT   (*right*)
["Commodore" Vanderbilt]
(1794–1877)
Capitalist, steamship and railroad owner;
consolidated New York Central system
Engraving by Alexander H. Ritchie

419
CALVERT VAUX   (*left*)
(1824–1895)
Landscape architect, planned parks in New
York City

420
HONUS WAGNER   (*right*)
[John Peter Wagner; Hans Wagner]
(1874–1955)
Baseball shortstop, charter member of Base-
ball Hall of Fame

421
LILLIAN D. WALD (*left*)
(1867–1940)
Social worker, reformer; founded Henry
Street Settlement, New York
Courtesy Henry Street Settlement House

422
LEW WALLACE (*right*)
[Lewis Wallace]
(1827–1905)
Union general in Civil War, diplomat;
author of *Ben Hur*
Photograph by Napoleon Sarony

423
ARTEMAS WARD (*left*)
(1727–1800)
Revolutionary general, Congressman
Painting by Charles Willson Peale. Courtesy Independence National Historical Park

424
BOOKER TALIAFERRO
WASHINGTON (*right*)
(1856–1915)
Educator, writer, lecturer; established Tuskegee Institute

425
GEORGE WASHINGTON (*left*)
(1732–1799)
President of the United States, 1789–1797
Painting by Gilbert Stuart

426
MARTHA WASHINGTON (*right*)
[Mrs. George Washington, Mrs. Martha
Custis, nee Martha Dandridge]
(1732–1802)
First lady, 1789–1797
Painting by Charles Willson Peale. Courtesy Independence National Historical Park

427
ANTHONY WAYNE (*left*)
["Mad Anthony" Wayne]
(1745–1796)
Revolutionary general, Congressman
Painting attributed to James Sharples, Sr. Courtesy Independence National Historical Park

428
DANIEL WEBSTER (*right*)
(1782–1852)
Lawyer, orator, U.S. Senator, Congressman; Secretary of State under W. H. Harrison, Tyler, and Fillmore
Courtesy New-York Historical Society

429
NOAH WEBSTER (*left*)
(1758–1843)
Lexicographer, grammarian, writer; a founder of Amherst College
Painting attributed to James Sharples, Sr. Courtesy Independence National Historical Park

430
GIDEON WELLES (*right*)
(1802–1878)
Republican leader, Secretary of the Navy under Lincoln and Andrew Johnson
Engraving by J. M. Butler

431
BENJAMIN WEST (*left*)
(1738–1820)
Painter
Painting by Gilbert Stuart

432
GEORGE WESTINGHOUSE (*right*)
(1846–1914)
Inventor, manufacturer; organized Westinghouse Electric Co.

433
PHILLIS WHEATLEY *(left)*
(c. 1753–1784)
Poet, freed slave

434
JAMES ABBOTT McNEILL
WHISTLER *(right)*
(1834–1903)
Painter, etcher
Courtesy Eric Schaal

435
WALT WHITMAN *(left)*
[Walter Whitman]
(1819–1892)
Poet
Courtesy Library of Congress, Brady-Handy Collection

436
ELI WHITNEY *(right)*
(1765–1825)
Inventor of the cotton gin; pioneer firearms
manufacturer
*Engraved by D. C. Hinman from a painting by
Charles B. King*

437
JOHN GREENLEAF WHITTIER
(left)
(1807–1892)
Poet

438
KATE DOUGLAS WIGGIN *(right)*
[nee Kate Douglas Smith]
(1856–1923)
Writer, leader in kindergarten movement;
wrote *Rebecca of Sunnybrook Farm*

439
ELLA WHEELER WILCOX (*left*)
[nee Ella Wheeler]
(1850–1919)
Journalist, poet

440
WOODROW WILSON (*right*)
[Thomas Woodrow Wilson]
(1856–1924)
President of the United States, 1913–1921
Courtesy New-York Historical Society

441
Mrs. WOODROW WILSON (*left*)
[nee Ellen Louise Axson]
(1860–1914)
First lady, 1913–1914
Courtesy Library of Congress

442
Mrs. WOODROW WILSON (*right*)
[Mrs. Edith Bolling Galt; nee Edith Bolling]
(1872–1961)
First lady, 1915–1921
Photograph by Arnold Genthe. Courtesy Princeton University Library

443
JOHN WINTHROP (*left*)
(1588–1649)
First governor of Massachusetts Bay Colony
Engraved by Frederick Girsch from a painting attributed to Van Dyck

444
OLIVER WOLCOTT (*right*)
(1726–1797)
Revolutionary general, signer of Declaration of Independence; Governor of Connecticut
Painting by Ralph Earle. Courtesy Connecticut State Library

445
FRANK LLOYD WRIGHT *(left)*
(1867–1959)
Architect

446
ORVILLE WRIGHT *(right)*
(1871–1948)
Aviation pioneer
Courtesy Meserve Collection

447
WILBUR WRIGHT *(left)*
(1867–1912)
Aviation pioneer
Courtesy Meserve Collection

448
BRIGHAM YOUNG *(right)*
(1801–1877)
Mormon leader, established the Mormon
Church in Utah
Courtesy Church of Jesus Christ of Latter-Day Saints

449
CY YOUNG *(left)*
[Denton True Young]
(1867–1955)
Baseball pitcher, member of Baseball Hall
of Fame
Courtesy National Baseball Hall of Fame

450
FLORENZ ZIEGFELD *(right)*
(1869–1932)
Theatrical producer
Courtesy Museum of the City of New York